THE WILD YONDER

A wholly owned subsidiary of **TBN**

The Wild Yonder

Trilogy Christian Publishers

A Wholly Owned Subsidiary of Trinity Broadcasting Network

2442 Michelle Drive

Tustin, CA 92780

Copyright © 2022 by Kelly Young Bennett

For information, address Trilogy Christian Publishing
Rights Department, 2442 Michelle Drive, Tustin, Ca 92780.
Trilogy Christian Publishing/ TBN and colophon are trademarks
of Trinity Broadcasting Network.

For information about special discounts for bulk purchases,
please contact Trilogy Christian Publishing.

Manufactured in the United States of America

10 9 8 7 6 5 4 3 2 1

Library of Congress Cataloging-in-Publication Data is available.

ISBN: 978-1-68556-076-8

ISBN: 978-1-68556-077-5

In memory of

Chong Hyo Nam

A man of honor, integrity, and courage

and

Dedicated to

Dong Soon Bae

A woman of love, sacrifice, and perseverance

CONTENTS

LOVE and FRIENDS

SEASONS, PLACES and THINGS

HUMOR

PASSING THOUGHTS

SPIRITUAL

LOVE and FRIENDS

MAXI

In the corner of a metal cage,
  By a little, dimly lit window hole,
Thou cowered as hope and love fled.
  Beyond reach and grasp,
A crushed kindred spirit groaned and mourned.

As thy eyes disappeared into the blackhole emptiness,
  Voices echoed in solemn somber silence,
Thy frozen ears shivered in fear and despair.

Called by the name "Maxi,"
  Thou were etched eternally
In the place of no return
  Till a gentle sweet breath tiptoed
Into your death scorned realm, and whispered,
  "My sweet, sweet darling Maxi,
Come out, come out to me and live!"

Carried away in the wings
  Of tender endearment and love sickness,
Thou took a mighty leap of courage and curiosity
  Unto millions of heartfelt embraces.
"I shall treasure this moment unto the utterances
  Of my last breath," so promised.

Thy emerald crystalline eyes,
  An ever-expanding gateway,
Are a wondrous and magnificent starry universe,
  Bringing forth much amusement and joy to bear.

Thy symphony of thunderous meows and purrs
　　Crushes all opposing sound waves into a dust of void.
Thy ears twinkle and waltz whirly
　　For a scrumptious delicacy of tasty morsels,
Howbeit, none dared to invade his precious realm,
　　For he is the new king of Shangri-La.

What a delightful tiny bundle of vivacity
　　That mesmerizes souls a million times over,
And bears a whole world of mine
　　Beyond depth, width, and height! Indeed, he is.

THE BLISS

How blissful is the instant fiery ardor,
　　Encircling my frozen mortal agony
In the night of a dead winter.

A much-cherished caress and embrace
　　Of thine brings forth the springs of euphoria,
Blanketing all corners of my universe.

A euphoric contentment and a beam of sunshine
　　Forever set in my soul and existence.
If I were to perish this instant howbeit,
　　I will, without tears and fear.

THE COMPANY OF LONESOME

Like a distant memory,
  The Lonesome greets a hesitant embrace.
Its bitter stiff air rejects all forms
  Of spoken words or a glimpse.

An eternal silence finally makes its first nod.
  The Lonesome swiftly takes my hand to its heart.
The cool teardrops cascading my fingers for ages,
  Stirring and fussing pitiful compassion beyond
  the passage.

The Lonesome whispers into my trembling eyes,
  "Before thee, the death angel was nigh."

Come. Come my dear, close your eyes.
  Rest thy heavy heart upon mine bosom tonight.
Cleave unto me and stay a while without hindrance.
  Let us wipe our tears of sorrowness.
Let the time pass without disturbance.

Like a distant memory,
  Let there be fervent embraces
Till such a time of company again comes.

EVERMORE

Bathed in the glorious Spring light,
  The sultry scent of gardenia
Almost seduces my spirit into a kiss,
  But your brushing kiss on my brow
Is evermore better.

Showered in the Summer morning beams,
  The brilliant waves of crystal and pearl,
Breaking from the sea of blades,
  Almost quenches my thirst for comfort,
But your tears of endearment and kindness
  Are evermore better.

Wrapped in the Autumn gowns,
  The infinite colors of heaven and earth
Almost dazzles my eyes to wander,
  But your tender embrace of love
Is evermore better.

Flown in the Winter twilight wings,
  The purest fairy dust of serenity
Almost intoxicates my soul to sleep,
  But your soft breath on my bosom
In the night of the dead slumber
  Is evermore better.

SWEET MAXI, SWEET MAXI

The worldly wicked web
    Entangles my conscience and sub,
Shackled with thousands of sinking chains,
    Into the merciless abyss of void and strains.

Shadowy armies of luminous eyes
    Of ominous death's rays
Paralyzes my existence.
    O where forth flee from these miseries?

Then a familiar warm spirit encompasses me:
    His silky whiskers softly tickle my feet,
His wooly tail gently anchors my leg,
    His emerald crystalline eyes beg
Of great adventures and exposé.

And like a battle-scarred warrior's vows,
    Magnificent pink paws shred the mouse
Into a thousand chips of blue.

When the evil reluctantly retreats into the shrouds,
    The happy head, riding on the soft cotton field clouds,
Lays his fuzzy flesh next to my beaten body,
    Summoning gentle waves of a purring lullaby,
And bringing my soul a most intoxicating bliss and peace.

Oh, my Maxi, sweet Maxi,
    My valiant rescuer and protector of sanity!
Stay with me forever, my Maxi, sweet Maxi.

MEOW 1

I fear them all-seeing sparkling glass eyes,
    Hunting every step of mine from far away.
Even now at my door threshold,
    I see marbles of two.

The eyes of the darkest winter night
    Seize every fiber of mine until his soft roar,
"Meow! Here I am! Where have you been?
    I am hungry. Where is my toy? Hello! Here I am!"

MEOW 2

Like a hollow cloud thrashing about the winds in all
directions,
    So is my heart devoid, deprived, and desolate
Of butter-soaked shrimp, "Meow!"

FEAST OF MAXI

Beyond the white fence,
    Two love birds madly feast
On the grains of all pleasures
    Over a glass of Chardonnay.

Laying on his throne, Maxi
    Feasts on his daily delight
With his eyes, a gate to the soul,
    On the pair of birds in euphoria.

MY DEAREST

My dearest softly kisses my brow,
    Planting the scent of the fairest
Lilies of the valley in my soul.

A thousand mountains and seas stand
    In between our paths,
Yet endearing memories bridge us
    As one, even as melancholy souls.

The somber shadows of your footsteps
    Are the sublime sunshine to my soul
As the ill dreams of yours are better than
    The joyous reality of others.

Send the winds of your precious scent
    Over the mountains and seas!
So shall my soul live once more,
    One more sweet hour of a dream,
A dream far too soon flees my grasp.

My dearest softly kisses my brow,
    Ushering the memories of the fairest
Lilies of the valley into my soul.

MY SWEET PIE

You are the pie in the sky.
    A masterpiece made in Heaven.
Made just for my soul, my soul only,
    Very temperamental, but sweet.

Trails of a savory scent on the wings
    Of a shadow on Jacob's ladder
In the misty moonless night sky
    Softly knock on my window.

A velvety voice like a melted sea of butter
    Moistens my throat in ecstasy,
Taking away my breath in a whiff of bliss,
    I am in the sky with my Sweet Pie.

EVER SINCE

Ever since you journeyed
    To Happy Mountain (as you called it),
My lion heart shattered
    In a million pieces of anguish.
Many flown away in grievous winds
    Over the mountains and seas,
But some were held back
    By reluctant red silk threads.

My bleeding and tattered heart sank
   Into the deep ever since.
The relentless waves of torment
   Pounded my beached heart
On the darkest shore alone.
   Your mortal farewell cruelly deprived this world
Of your sacrificial honor, courage, integrity, and love.

Even the dreams of you fled me in horror.
   Forgotten and abandoned memories
Of you haunt my soul ever since.
   Only a bitter tear-drenched pillow
Comforts me, nothing more.
   Oh, my dear, dear father, how my heart tormented
For your missing so long!

On one cool autumn night, a sea mount breeze
   Knocks on my forlorn grey heart.
And says, "My dear, my dear,
   I have seen the pieces of your lion heart
In Happy Mountain, in the hands of your beloved."

My ancient spirit awakens and races
   As the reminiscence of my dear father
Floods my heart once again.
   Oh, how I wish my head in your bosom
To feel your heartbeats one more time.
   I long for your gentle cool stroke
On my feverish bristles, and my jubilant soul
   On the Happy Mountain trail.
Oh, my dear, dear father, how my heart aches
   For your dream ever since.

IN THE BLINK OF AN EYE

Your radiant smile
  Of the brightest star
Lightens my bleak sorrow.

Your sweet words
  Of contentment stirs
A little joy in my heart.

Your soft caresses on my head,
  Tender and loving
Memories of the past,
  Floods my spirit with
Laughter and tears of endearment.

And these are the treasures,
  Irreplaceable blessings
Of yesterday.

Today, your smile is frozen
  Like a stone of steel
Of the deep earth,
  Bringing forth eternal anguish.

Your words of cruelty,
  Silent and void to my wailings,
Cuts my soul a million times over.

Your bitter cold flesh upon
    My fiery bosom numbs my spirit
With an utter terror and agony
    Of this world and beyond,
For I died today with you.

Do not wait for me, my love.
    Do not hasten my footsteps,
For I shall be with you
    In the blink of an eye
Just as you have departed
    My world of nothingness
In the blink of an eye.

MY LOVE

Deep as the breath of the moon,
    Wide as the wind's castle,
Tall as the throne of the Almighty,
    So shall be my love for you,
And yours forever.

COLD FEET

Once cold feet, always cold feet
    At times on the first kiss of a sweet,
Sometimes at the wedding vows of eternity,
    But most of all, in the embrace of a lonely.

But sometimes, in the company of a frosty
    Breath of wintery blight,
Cold feet swiftly kiss the belly
    Of a miserably sweltering knight.

Bringing much solace to the night,
    Cold feet and the knight
Are finally warmed, cooled, and united
    In the most blessed contrite.

SLEEPLESS NIGHT

More enchanting and subliming are the sleepless nights
    Under the mesmerizing moon beam blanketing my
    world
In the bosom of the sweet-smelling lily of the valley.

The summoned ancient memories of the endearing one,
    Gone astray and lost in the world of concrete jungles,
Slowly stirs the fire seed in my heartache of longing.

The rekindled spirit of my lovely one warms my heart,
   A moment too easily led astray by the drops of the
   moon-lit dew.
But my darling, fly back to me whilst my heart awaits still,

For the way is adorned with angelic waves of solemn songs.
   The pearly dew of my tears luminate in the silver lights,
And my heart sings and dances for your shadow's return.

AN ELEPHANT'S MEMORY

As the fingers tiptoe on the ivory keys
   In the cool evening by the moon river,
A lone shadow joins the stage.

When the Moonlight Sonata gently echoes the water,
   The shadow flaps its leathery wings,
And hugs its ivory fangs dearly.

As the night's crescendo breaks the silence,
   Tears well in the deep winter sockets, and
Trickle down the dusty weathered hide.
Remembering the ghosts of the past,
   The mighty giant stands still
In the melody of a somber death, or not.

THE SUBSTANCE OF TIME

Like a flea fleeing in a blink of an eye,
    Time flies in stealth mode
Wherever the destination may be,
    For it tells and shows no souls.

Whenever the sneaky time travels to and fro,
    The strength and beauty of an innocent youth
Keeps a faithful companion, and the thrill of the chase
    Keeps up with the fleeting time.

Fifty winters since the chase,
    A reflection on the mirror tells no discretion,
And the utterances of it are timeless
    As it shouts, "Holy mackerel! Holy cow!"

The stolen time teases my melancholy soul.
    But my lovely says to my blushing ears,
"Mackerel or cow not, you are still the apple of my eye.
    Your substance is even sweeter than ever more."

THE PLIGHT OF TWO FRIENDS

The old twisted lone Juniper tree
  On the rugged sandstone rocks
Stands firm against the wind of travail
  To hold and shelter a visiting friend,
A winged creature from high above the soaring clouds,
  From a weary flight against the same wind of travail.

Envious of the courtship of the two,
  Blows a mighty gale upon the ancient tree and young
  fowl.
Over and over, the tree whips, and the fowl's talons
  Dig hard against the rocks.
The wings of the young, and the limbs of the old
  Silently endure the maddening scourges of the wind.

Suddenly the dust settles, and the air is calm.
  The wind of Jealousy finally retires for the moment.
The fowl stretches its tattered and dusted wings
  On the old, twisted limbs of the dearest,
Savoring a sweet moment of salutation,
  Before the tempestuous antipathy catches her breath
  again.

MAXI IN TRAINING

A smart but frisky cat named Maxi is in training.
  Scrumptious tuna treats are given
Every time the bell dings.
  Ding! Ding! Ding!
And his eyes widen like a baseball.
  Oh boy, is he ever a changed cat!

A very clever cat named Maxi is now busy training
  His human butler again.
His paws fly like a mad Ninja's shooting stars.
  Ding! Ding! Ding!
And here I come with the treats.
  Oh boy, am I ever regretting it!

THE CLOUD LADDER

Lend me a Cloud Nine ladder to the moon,
  For my panting heart is a blue ruin.
Lift me up beneath the winds of a blazing spite,
  For I long to quench your luminance tonight
Before the winds carry me to the blackness of the pit.

MAXIMUS LANDING

In the land where King Maximus is the ferocious warrior,
    A sea of silk bedding awaits his anytime slumbers
While a heavenly feathered breeze shoos away all whispers.
    Every soul breathes carefully, not to awaken the royal
    highness.
His ears hear all, even the lurking clouds in the darkness.

Meanwhile, the ever-faithful butler combs all corners of the
earth
    To gather the finest meat and drinks, all for the high birth,
For his appetite changes with the tides of the ocean.
    Yesterday, Trout Meuniere, today, Peking Duck
    blackened.
Tomorrow, no one ever is certain.

As the sweet slumber retreats, the butler cowers
    In the chamber of ominous murmurs and growls.
Quickly, the fitting feast begins with watchful eyes.
    The King smiles, his fangs skewing the demise,
As his tongue rips the flesh from the bones.

Drenched in fear, the court jester moans
    As the last morsel is gulped down.
The King's beastly gaze now steady on his trembling clown.
    Nothing can go wrong or be forgiven.
It would be the moment not to be forgotten.

The King descends from the mighty setting,
    His magnificent claws quickly approaching,
Coiling and clenching his subject with his furry stinger,
    He lets out a "MeOw!", the infamous roar.
The King's raised tail is dancing high
    As a happily exhausted butler takes a deep sigh.

SEASONS, PLACES and THINGS

AN ENCHANTED ENCOUNTER

While on a journey at the foothills of Jiri Mountain,
    A splendid appearance,
A tender white flower on the edge of Seldom path,
    Caresses my ankle and arrests my heart.

A gentle cool breeze dances with the flower,
    Enticing my fluttered heart even more
Like a long-lost endearing reunion
    Of silent greetings of gladness and happiness,
And of tender kindred spirit kisses.

Together, we marvel and soak in
    A masterpiece of a sunset glory
Whilst a little regret creeps in
    As our time of departure approaches.

You reluctantly see me off on heavy footstep.
    You comfort me, making joyful promises:
After a season of winter and slumber,
    I shall be here with the thought
Of another enchanted encounter.

MISTY FOG

Wherefore hast thou come?
　　To play hide and seek amongst the solitude of Junipers?

Has thou found the secret of the wild blue yonder?
　　Or has thou hidden the pearls of ancient wisdom?

"Not today," the misty fog whispers
　　As it flies away weeping softly.

THE RETURN OF THE SUNFLOWER

Suddenly, the black wind of trickery
　　Seeps into my heavenly sunshine.
Whilst wondering and doubting,
　　The fiery sun retreats into darkness,
Taking away my blows despite
　　My earnest begging and protests.

The soft wind of warmth brushes my crowns.
　　I wonder if it is a dream or reality?
Not a dream as the trickster wind turns violent,
　　And the wet gale cuts my flesh a thousand times.

My love, where art thou, my sunshine?
For I am sinking into the abyss of blue.
When will thou again return to me?
    Weary in hopeless despair, desire, and vanity,
Even time has betrayed and fled me.

The tenacious dark wet path stalks me still,
    Drenching my heart's desires to escape.
Will this be the end of me?

Behold! In the distance, in the broken sky,
    My brave sunshine writhes away
To dazzle my eyes once again.
    Come hither, come forth my love,
For here I am still panting.

My firefly love, with a sincere apology,
    Rekindles my heart once again.
He softly opens my eyes, heart, and spirit
    Unto the glorious golden light,
For I am called the Flower of the Sun.

ANGEL'S LANDING

Whispers of a secret legend
   By a very froward wind
Speaks of an ancient city
   Deep within Zion:
Red rock towers and spires,
   A maze below of razor thin straits,
And the place of the narrows.

It is a marvelous tale of a place,
   A portal to a majestic realm
In the midst of Heaven and earth.
   It is Jacob's ladder, a landing
For winged immortal hosts,
   And a getaway from the deep
Of torrid sins and torment,
   Called Angel's Landing.

Carried by the wind,
   The legend was sowed
In the grievous mortal's heart
   Of the Conqueror of all vanities.
Like the relentless surf
   Breaking the shore,
The filthy shadows of the greediest pride
   Trampled the splendors' glory
Of a heaven on earth.
   The angels retreated,
Saving the landing.

The Angel's Landing of Zion,
   A foretell of an awe
And a magnificent divinity,
   Still stands a work of perfect wonder
At the end of a narrow strait,
   Endowing the mortals' spirits
A little glimpse of Heaven
   Time after time.

STARRY SKY

As the rising red globe perches
   On the Eastern Mountain sky,
The descending curtain is upon the beloved,
   A star of spectacle, the Starry Sky.

Prompting a much-deserved rest
   After much intense fireworks,
The star takes its adieu bow.

But the show must go on
   As a fervent demanding audience awaits,
Waiting on the other side of the stage
   For the beloved star to reappear.

Prompting the raising of the curtain upon the beloved,
   The glorious symphony of the Starry Sky
Commands the opulent center stage once again.

Basking in the showers of adoration,
   Full of wondrous glory and splendid melody,
The Starry Sky spreads its wings of sparkling gems.
   Bravo, Bravo! The show must go on!

DRAGON OF KEA

A far away Isle holds a great mystery called Kea
    Of whom a whirlwind reveals a legendary lore of
    perilous terror
From sea to sea and crater to crater.
    The tale of a molten venom fire breathing drag on lady,
And a roaming sea of molten rock lizards,
    Perched high up in the black stone mountain.
Here, only a few brave souls dare to breathe.

As the misty fog flees the mountain,
    The shadows and silhouettes of the feared one,
And the fury scorned lady's lair grows,
    Arresting the hearts of mighty men furthermore.

Through the razer cut cavern mazes,
    Upon every burnt shrapnel,
Behold, the scales of slithery snakes.
    On the hazy horizon of reptilian vertebrates
Are thousands of blackened headless limbs
    Frozen still in fiery stones.

No soul would dare venture into her lair,
    But, only from afar, watch
The great dragon lady
    Lay still in her cavern
Till her furor is no longer contained.

As the earth rumbles,
    A great thunder and smoke awaken.
The lady exhales her poisonous breath,
    And spews her gurgling blood of wrath
From her bosom core of molten sea,
    Ready to consume all.

None dare slay the great dragon of the Kea,
    For she is the lord of the land and its soul.
In the land of a great mystery and awesome beauty,
    The headless limbs would concur a thousand times.

THE MONA

The cool soothing mystic streams of thy exhale
  Maketh all souls forthwith quicken with such a feast.
The fruit of thy breath brings forth
  The most excellent pearl strings of the dawn dew
Much esteemed by hungry and thirsty souls of the earth
below.

Like a chary bride about to raise a veil of a great secret,
  Thou carefully uncloak an ever-luminous face
For admirers of all ages and nations
  To lighten their dreary soul,
hasten their weary steps,
  And uphold their spirit heaven bound.

And for the glorious redemption from folly and sins of
the day,
  Thy silver wings carry the yoke of the slumber souls
Across the heaven all night long.

As the last vapors of thy breath vanish in the horizon,
  The earth and heaven, full of milk and honey,
At last, morph from nothingness into an existence
  Of magnificent grace and power.

The day is tolerable because the joyous memories
  Of thy gentle fragrant zephyrs etched
In our soul bringeth much comfort and peace.

WAITING FOR MISS DAISY

Freddie was indeed the most whirlwind bird in the grove.
   But for Daisy, he was an old fashion love,
For she was fair and much sought after.
   Before the sunrise, Freddie would fluster.
Before the mirror, Freddie would rehearse.
   All for Daisy because she was an irresistible force.

With a buffet of the finest grains on a platter,
   Guarded from a pesky plunder,
He rolled out the red carpet for Daisy,
   And gently called for his lady.
And waited for her accession,
   Waiting and waiting with affection since dawn.

At dusk was Daisy's grand appearance,
   Much to Freddie's perseverance.
Feasting on the finest meals on display,
   Daisy sang praises of the enchanted soiree.
Freddie's burning heart embraced every note,
   For Morrow's press is still far from the quotes.

THE FOUR HORSE RIDERS

The colorless horse rider gently treads the meadow,
    For the babes of earth slumber.
Howbeit, one brave soul breaks out of the cocoon,
    And morphs into a splendid array of infinite colors.
A sweet gentle breath of one brave maiden called Anastase
    Entices the horse rider to rest in her warm bosom.

The red horse rider scorches horizon to horizon,
    His hellish breath suffocating the hours and days.
A subtle lucid sea breeze teases the red horse rider,
    Should I stay or go?
The tears of joy pour down from Heaven
    As the red horse rider says, "Yes, do stay."

The pale horse rider chases
    Away the winds of all colors and shapes,
Thrashing poor souls into dismay and disarray.
    A lone leaf shakes violently in fear,
Clinging against the mighty gales
    And angry whips of the pale horse rider.
In time, the last brave leaf joins the bottom of the forest,
    Longing to see the Savior in due time.

The white horse rider storms into the field,
    Followed by a million sparkles of white dust,
Bringing in both awe and terror.
    The souls of the earth lay quiet and asleep
As the lullaby sung by a lone voice
    Is carried away in the white wind.
Rest, rest assure my soul,
    For it is the season and time
Till the white horse rider passes
    Over the foothills of the mountain.

REMEMBER THIS DAY

As the Moon and Earth swoon the Sun,
    Since the beginning of the foundation,
The curse of the day has begun.

Remember me this day,
    Yesterday prays
As the dawn breaks for Today.

For Today may not be sustained,
    And Tomorrow may not be entertained,
But I was the Today and Tomorrow wished.

THE SUN QUEEN

One furious day in August,
    All was quiet and still, except for
A lady in a blazing red chariot
    Racing across the sky
With the whips of fiery scorpions
    Of excruciating torture,
Of sting and thirst,
    Which would undo any mortal body.

Nothing and no soul can appease
    The burning fever
Of the lady of furor hissing.
    All is quiet and still until
Her blood thirst is quenched,
    Her red dusted chariot
And the blood-stained whips
    Are ready to be washed again.

As shadows of her crowns
    Cast brilliant trails
Of reds, blues, and golds on the horizon,
    Bewitched and mesmerized
Souls of the earth and heaven
    Bid the Sun queen a farewell
With marvel and adoration
    Before her furor flares again.

DANCERS OF HEAVEN

Have you ever seen
   The ballet of a silky frond's feathers
Dancing in the symphony of a sea breeze
   Under mystic golden beams,
Casting graceful waves
   Of curves and turns?

You, my dear, should consider this
   As it is ever more mesmerizing than
Any magnificent dancer under
   The supreme lights or direction
Of mortal minds and spirit,
   For it is Heaven made.

TALES OF THE SEASONS

As the Big Dipper gathers the Milky Way in the heavens,
  The earthly creatures embrace for the timely arrival
Of the one with a tempestuous and bewitching spirit.

He will descend upon the mountains and the valleys
  With a death-breeding frozen breath, a blackened soul
  of the deep earth,
And a voice of a great void uttering nothingness.

The Winter King has taken the reign of the earth
  With an army of terrible display and power,
And none dares to challenge this cruelty beyond.

But in the secret chamber, the King weeps
  For his sweet but fearsome love,
Knowing her fiery passion will devour his icy soul.

The irresistible love of the Winter King and Sun Queen,
  Forged long ago in the deepest chamber,
Finds its only solace in a birth called Spring.

When the child Spring takes its first breath,
  The King retreats and watches from a distance,
A heartwarming union of His love, and child.

The King sheds his frozen tears from the sky
  To remind them of his touch, scent, and sound
Of a loving soul who misses them dearly.

PART 2

Amidst the showers of starry sparkles in the white field,
   The Winter King catches a glimpse of a mystic shadow.
Warm and soft, she tenderly caresses the intrigued King.

Her voice is like a gentle stream in the secret garden.
   Her scent of Jasmine and lavender wades heavenly songs.
Her illuminating eyes turn the darkest chamber into a
dreamy lair.

Lady Mona, a maiden of the Sun Queen, seduces the King
   Into her milky bosom and fills his desires to no end.
Thus, the forbidden love of the unfortunate Maiden and the
King.

Autumn, a most flamboyant yet tormented soul of the
seasons,
   And the love child of Moon and Winter,
Patiently waits, enduring the wrath of the Sun Queen.

At last, Lady Mona boldly visits Autumn in the cool of the
evening,
   Embracing the child in the warm glows of affection
   and love,
She softly wipes away the tears of anguish and sorrow.

The Winter King takes the child by the hand
   Into his own bedchamber, and lets him rest
Til their heartstrings are strengthened again.

The Winter King gently summons an angelic lullaby
   To console the bleeding heart of Lady Mona,
And to comfort Autumn that they are not forgotten.

PART 3

Her bosom is like waves of the ocean before the storm,
  Calm and serene like heaven above the sea of clouds.
So quiet is the breath of the Sun Queen, it is as if the
world has stopped turning.

A sudden gale from the pine forest rocks the bedchamber
of the Queen,
  And quickly runs away as the Queen awakes to her fury.
Her chest, full of fire reeds, is ready to unleash her
consuming wrath on any soul.

Then one little fire seed secretly takes refuge in the womb of
the Queen.
  For months, the little spirit of fire unravels the womb of
  the Sun Queen
Until the day of great pain spits the Queen beyond her
pangs of furor.

Born of an inferno spirit and begotten of her mother's
blazed heart,
  A spitfire called Summer breathes her first flame in the
  arms of the Queen.
A wild child of the Queen, unwanted by her and her
mysterious lover.

Sometimes, Summer gathers winds of all direction in the
ocean,
   Stirring and churning of the great sea floors and waves
The earth mourns, unaware of Summer's motive: a
cleansing of an old stale life.

Sometimes, Summer runs wildly barefooted in the forest
without hesitation,
   Leaving behind her path of blood sweat, blisters and
   burnt ashes.
The earth groans, unaware of Summer's intent: the
beginning of a new life.

Sometimes, Summer is adored by her admirers all day and
all night,
   Igniting the fire of passion within, making Summer's
   love zealous yet innocent.
The earth rejoices, unaware of Summer's desire: desperately
seeking her own love life.

A MIND OF FOG

A pair of footprints on a lonely path
    Parades at a snow blossomed dawn.
"Where have you gone, my darling?"
    Whispers the bashful Fog of East.
The only reply is the sound of his own breath.

The faint traces of a fawn, fond of the grove,
    Stirs happy memories of the past season.
Carefully treading, not disturbing the slumbering field,
    The mystified Fog looks left and right, up, and down,
Only to see a red globe perched on the white horizon.

The blinding sun beams, brilliant and warm,
    To melt any cruel heart and its memory,
Even the disappearing footprints of the darling.
    The Fog swoons around and around,
Only to see the zealous sun climbing steeply even more.

The dampened spirit of the weary Fog
    Rejects the Sun's solace and embrace
Until the silhouette of his darling, from a shadow,
    Greets the bashful Fog, and the dazzling sun light.
Only then the Fog takes a much-needed rest and slumber.

THE GREAT SKY ROAMER

All eyes are fixated on an old timer
   As his dusty scarred talons are carefully perched
At the edge of a rocky cliff.

Thunderous and fearsome wings of yesterday
   Are today's bruised and marred wings,
Gathering unknown anxiety and fears.

Without the feathers of the wind,
   The predator becomes the prey,
And a great feast for his lucky foe.

The shadow cautiously unfolds its wings,
   A truly magnificent sight and awe
Of a monstrous winged raptor.

Tasting the air of hesitance beneath,
   The trembling feathers fold again
While troubled eyes search for a little comfort.

The seasoned vulture flutters his feathers once again.
   Again, again, and again like it is his virgin flight.
All eyes silently wait and wait for the old timer's fate.

Suddenly, the great sky roamer dives into the ravine,
   And barely swoops around the edge of the rock!
But the steady wings steer up towards heaven.

All eyes follow the wings of the free.
   Encircling, and entailing the patriarch
Are happy merry go arounds in the sky.

THE LAIR OF LADY M.

It is a place beyond the red mountains
    Where clouds hesitate to venture
And the mist hides in the dens.

It is a place where the sun does not set
    As its merciless army of fiery darts
Devour all, even ashes.

It is a place where a time traveler
    Wanders in just to be
Lost and forgotten.

It is a place where the desolate
    Begs for a companion
Even for a split second.

All abhor the place
    Of the cursed and God forsaken
Except for the mischievous Lady Mirage.

HALO OF THE MOON

How the bittersweet embracing and wailing
    Drowned my weary soul and wrecked my brined spirit!
Summoned is the distant yet blissful memory
    Of my daughter born of heartstrings
In the battlefield of charred skulls and bones.

Oh, how the fountain of moonlit tears
    Ruptured at the utterance of your name.
Ayla, Ayla, my darling Ayla,
    A name born of sorrow,
Weaved with pangs of woe and heartaches.

Sacrificial offerings and innocent prey were you and I;
    Lost and sinking in the wretched sea
Of bloodied corpses and gores of hell,
    Accompanied by a demonic glee of warmongers,
And blood-soaked whips of thorns and thistle.

But you, my bright eyes brimming with dew, found me
    In the death den choked with hissing vipers,
In the cradle of my rancid body and spirit,
    In the stenches of agony and an opened sepulcher,
As found I the hope of salvation at last!

Because of your unfaltering love and faith
    In the midst of Hades' belly,
Carried down the silver stream of redemption was my soul.
    No matter where it flows henceforth,
My soul shall rest in divine peace and sweet hours.

My eyes shall not inherit dirt,
    My mouth shall not be meat for worms,
And my bone marrow shall not suffer from fiery darts
    When my sweet darling Ayla is in my bosom,
Wiping away all my tears and grief.

THE EPITOME OF MEN

Consider the great marvel and wonders of the desert,
    Three thousand years of secrets and treasures,
An epitome of men's endeavor and testimony,
    And an ancient city by the river Nile of Egypt.

The great pyramid, sky towering statues, and temples
    Are the works of demi-gods etched in the rock and sand,
All adorned with gold and precious metals,
    A relic of a bygone civilization.

A magnificent work of imagination and precision,
    Impossible to duplicate or replicate,
It is a truly glorious masterpiece under heaven,
    Yet they are the lost and forgotten works of men.

The tombs of the pharaohs, the gods of the Egyptians,
    Plundered by the hands of thieves,
Desecrated by the winds and rain,
    And cursed under the footsteps of their people.

The statues and temples of great kings and queens,
    Fallen and abused by the hands of their people,
Are blown away in the winds of fury
    To be trodden under the footsteps of beasts.

Now consider the infinite works of grace, life, and power
    Of the one true living God, who created all things
Under the heavens, in the heavens, and of the heavens,
    A glorious divinity of splendor on display.

The great architects and engineers of the Nile,
    In awe of the mysterious works
Of the sun, moon, and stars of the universe,
    Regarded not the Creator of these creations.

The curse of Egypt is the curse of humanity.
    Let us remember the great Nile,
And its fallacy of three thousand years and beyond,
    Even now as its fate continues.

THE FOUR WINDS

The East Wind

It is a place where the sky and sea secretly rendezvous,
    Where Neptune's throne rules the underworld,
And where solitude found my company a pleasure.

Then, out of nowhere, came the wind from the East
    With its claws, and a death grip on my throat
As the great sea opened his mouth below my feet.

Thrown into the void of abyss were my soul,
    Tossing and thrashing were my mortal body,
In all directions and all manners, judging my spirit terribly.

The East Wind's grin was etched on my mind as I
    Sunk into the black death-cloud pass,
But of eerie songs of calm and serene blues.

Drifted and carried about the tempestuous vortex,
    I prayed the Almighty God for His mercy and grace,
For I know who holds tomorrow and eternal.

My Lord, do not forsake thy love!
    Let the wrath of the Wind die and let thine peace find me.
Let my presence be pleasing to your sight.

I then heard the angelic voices in me,
    Calling my name above all names
As I fell asleep in the deep dreams of many pleasures.

The South Wind

A brine caked body was I beached on the shore.
　　The sun's zeal has eaten me alive. Moaning and
Groaning, ready to expire was my perilous breath.
　　Then from the Aeolus' cave, the South Wind heard my cry,
And felt pity and pondered on this grievous, mortal soul.

Escaping the watchful eyes of the wind god and its lair,
　　The Wind gathered a rolling sea of clouds unto him
And blew and blew them towards the sea and sky from the
mountain.
　　The brave clouds seduced the fiery Sun into a sweet
　　slumber.
Behind the veils of clouds, the chariot of fire stood still for
a moment.

I felt the cool sea breeze caressing my broken body,
　　The mighty king's shadow kissing my eyes,
Tears of the knights trickling down my mangled lips,
　　And soft echoes of the sea lullaby in my ears.
My last breath, at the threshold of Hades, slowly retreated.

Oh, South Wind, how forever I am grateful for your kindness,
　　Bearing the furies of Aeolus and Helios.
How shall I not offer my thanksgiving unto the Almighty
　　With a song of prayers for your safe return and welfare?
For thou hast considered and shielded my soul from the
furnace.

The North Wind

The reputation of the North Wind,
　　its relentless brutal tyranny and ghastly terror,
Has reached all corners of the earth and universe.

For that testimony, the North Wind is kept
　　In the iron cage all but for one season.
But madness has no regard for neither the place nor time.

While in Aeolus' cave, the North Wind conspires the
unthinkable.
　　At an opportune time, the Wind gathers its army,
Breaks out of the cavern, and hurls down beneath the realm
of clouds,
　　Ready to strike the unsuspecting suckling of Spring, one
　　more time.

The darkling death-breath of the North Wind threatens
the young blows
　　With the unmerciful wrath of a chokehold, squeezing
　　out the last exhale,
And drowning them in bitter cold sorrowness and death.
　　Once again, the wuthering height of a meadow is under
　　siege.

As the wind god is at his heels, the North Wind smirks,
　　Back in the cave, chained, and shackled for a season.
Left behind are the trails of perished young blooms of
Spring,
　　And the wailings for the untimely tragic loss of her
　　children.

The West Wind

The massacre of the North Wind has not escaped
 The minds of Zephyrus, recalling the frightened cries
Of the doom destined and perished blows
 Of his children of the innocent meadows.

The West Wind visits the chamber of the Sun.
 Lamenting for the loss and weary of his foe,
The Sun god whose slumber at its sweet hour
 Hastens his wake for the sake of the Spring.

Stretching his rays of a fervent radiance
 From the East Sea shores to the West mountains and
 beyond,
Piercing the darkness driven by the maddening menace,
 The West Wind blows a warm affection across the valley.

And the Sun's ardent firefly surges through,
 Through the veins of the downed blows.
And behold! The heirs of Springs are reborn again
 Under the gentle cradles of Zephyrus at last.

HUMOR

THE SLEEPY CLOUD

A sleepy cloud in Summer Sky
   Was napping in Sleepy valley.
A chilly wind from Chilly Mountain
   Awakened the cloud with a commotion
Because the wind wanted the same sweet spot!
   But the sleepy cloud blew the wind oft.
The angry wind blew the cloud far away.
   So far away, the wind swayed,
And the sleepy cloud dismayed.
   Now a castaway in the Winter Sky!
The sleepy cloud cried all the day,
   For he missed his Autumn Sky.

RODNEY

He was admired by all,
   For he was a master strutter
With magnificent feathers of rainbows.
   Ladies of all ages, color, and stature,
Flocked to his charm and swag.

His voice was like an ocean,
   Mighty sometimes, gentle sometimes,
Soothing all ears of the earth,
   And serenading all day long in the House of the Hen.

But most of all, he was a true gentleman
   Because he crows not at early dawn's light
To awake the morning glory of peace,
   Or the ladies' beauty sleep.

He was admired by all, a rooster named Rodney.
Born blind, no sun arises on his crown.
But all souls love him dearly,
For Rodney was a bird of discretion and discernment.
A bird of few words especially in the early morning.

CLOUD NINE

Neath the layers of cotton candy fluffs,
Are his core of memory foam buffs,
Are the envy of all heavenly puffs,
For theirs are hollow muffs.

Cloud Nine, a cloud of a fancy,
Is the apple in the eye of the sleepy
Sheep of a nightly jumpy journey.
One misadventure, the sleepy tumbles spirally
All the way down to an unfortunate folly.

For his puff is a glorious ride,
Swooning the sleepy sheep all night,
Resting soundly on the twilight,
On his magnificent cream puff of might.

THE TUESDAY THING

Through the shimmery veils,
    The Eastern dawn's showers of light
Cleanse away the night's mires
    As figments of ambrosial dreams
Refresh my soul, body, and spirit.

As a familiar sea birdsong tickles my ears,
    The lucid sea sultry scent
Stirs a recent happy memory
    Of my sweet Maxi, one basket of sunshine,
Pressing against my body,
    Wishing the moment to linger.

As a faint earth tremor approaches
    Closer and rapidly without a heartbeat,
Memories of the Tuesday Thing resurrect:
    The metal beast creeping in with
Bone breaking shark's steel teeth,
    And a suffocating phosphorus breath
With demonic screams of all hideous creatures.

Chasing away the songs and scent,
    The Tuesday Thing, full of wrath,
Provokes my sweet Maxi and I
    To seek a new refuge, but none avail.

The Tuesday Thing pulps away
    The wailing sea of green blades,
Thrashing limbs mercilessly and relentlessly,
    And forcing all beings into hiding.

When the final blade is cut down,
    The terror retreats with happy whistles and hums.
Deserted is the reminisce
    Of a bloody purge and carnage
With the strangely sweet scent of summer
    As a consolation and reminder.

As the calm and peace reclaim its realm,
    Oh, how we quickly forget the rage and atrocity
Of the Tuesday Thing's rampage
    Until the next memories' appointed time
Arrives on que, as always, in misery.

A SAD, ANGRY WIND

The Angry wind's heart was waft.
    He had a first date with the Lady Cloud Soft.
For a memorable first impression of himself,
    He redeemed a cheap but nice cologne for a change of whiff.

But before he could say, "Enchanté" to the Lady Cloud Soft,
    The Angry wind coughed, coughed, coughed,
And coughed until the Lady Cloud Soft was no longer aloft.
    The Angry wind was mournful that his date was too soft,
And for the cologne that was a knock-off.

FOOL'S ERRAND

The Fool says, "There is no air,
   For she cannot see."
The mischief Air says,
   "I have a secret chamber
Full of everlasting air for a penny."

The Fool says, "Here!
   Here is a penny for the air."
The mischief Air says,
   "Bring me a vessel, and I shall fill it to the rim."

The Fool says, "Here!
   Here is the vessel for the air.
Give her all of it, for she will fill it from head to toe."
   The mischief Air says,
"Here, here. Drink all of it whilst it lasts."

The Fool says, "When?
   When will she know when to get more?"
The mischief Air says,
   "Whenever you exhale, come, come with a penny."

MILADY FRIDAY

The thought of you, milady,
    Brings forth joyful hums and whistles
Back into my soul, and my feet in cloud nine.

But the all-seeing evil lord's eyes
    Lurk every corner by leaps and bounds
With a vicious hunting beast at his feet
    Ready to bound my free spirit.

As the hands of aging clocks creeps
    Closer to the top, the top of the wall,
All eyes, both good and bad,
    Freeze in suspense and terror.

At last! The last gong tolls,
    Breaking all shackles and chains of the evil lord.
Behold, your lovely shadows of adoration
    Finally emerge from the dungeon.

The clock tower dances and sings
    For your triumph proclamation,
And the evil lord cowers cowardly
    Behind the shadows of his beasts.

Milady Friday, you are the heroin of this world,
    And mine, over and over.
Thank God! It's Milady Friday!

AFTER THE FEAST

For my beautiful porcelain skin,
    Your firm caress and strokes of tenderness
Are bubbly for they do wonders
    As lavender-fragrant dew lathers
Under the stainless fountain of pure springs.

Each stroke taketh away
    The filth and grime of a fiery havoc
Engraved in my heart of ware.
    Many turn their blind eyes at the horrific sight,
But you rescue me from the sinkhole of pigswill.

Like the holy blood washes away the sins,
    So does my gory reminisce of gluttony sin
Under the gentle streams of pure water.
    Because of your love, I can face tomorrow again.
"Ahem, you missed a spot. Just a little flick of dry sauce."

HUFFING AND PUFFING

A little child, full of a haughty spirit,
   Rocks the limbs of an old frail tree,
Laughing, huffing, and puffing.
   The gentle spirit of the old grove
Groans and sighs for its broken limbs.

A mischievous wind from the ocean
   Blows in to rescue his dear friend.
The wind caresses the limbs of an old tree
   Whilst rocking the little child.

The child falls and runs to her mother.
   Pouting, huffing, and puffing,
The angry mother with a fiery wrath
   Readies herself to torch the old tree.

The old tree shudder in fear and terror,
   And cries out to his friend.
Roaring, huffing, and puffing,
   The angry wind blows and blows,
Taking the seed of fire in the air
   To the house of the mother and little child.

The child and the mother blow and blow.
   Crying, huffing, and puffing,
They blow to put out the smoke and flames.
   But the mischievous wind was so angry
That he blows and blows until the house burns down.

SWEET SINS

I am forever dreaming of lust,
　　Seven layers of a sweet cotton candy cake
Topped with fiery red strawberries swimming
　　In the rivers of creamy milk puffs and honey,
Swirling in the fairy dusted crowns of ecstasy.

Then the gloomy reality shows me
　　The buttery fat layers of a belly tummy
Dancing with every movement of gravity,
　　A reminder of the dreadful long shadows of the sins
Of a reckless night of sweet tooth temptations.

AKA MR. BUTTERBALL

Mr. Pride, dripping with the grease of arrogance,
　　Parades himself on the center stage
Like a peacock in a beauty pageant.

Missing the crack below,
　　Mr. Pride tumbles down, down, and down,
All the way down the lane like a butterball.

Licking off the dirt and grease,
　　Mr. Pride scrambles for a fan of assurance
To assure him that he is still perfect.

THE HAPPY SPARROWS PUB

A pub called the "Happy Sparrows"
    In a bustling street hub
Where all shapes, sizes, and colors of wings
    Gather and merry for a season
Until the Captains call for the tour of duty.

When the clock tower tolls its bells,
    The race is on! Frenzy wheels flying,
Circling the airfield of chaos and panic.
    All souls are confused and bemoaning
At the hands of flustered guards at the gates.

Not for the fainthearted, the battle continues.
    Precious cargos are thrown in the air,
Tossed about in all directions and places.
    Some are lost forever, and others are bruised.
When will be the end of this wretched journey?

At last, the big bird is in the air!
    Mortal cargo is stowed in row after row.
Bitter drinks and stale bread never tasted so good.
    The gentle humming makes one almost forgetful of
The straps and chains on the weary flesh and souls.

In a bustling street hub,
    A pub called the "Happy Sparrows"
Greets all weary refugees and guards from the battlefield.
    At last, happy hour is here, too sordidly good to pass
The acid drinks, to wash away the insanity until the next toll.

LOUIE THE PINEAPPLE

Ah, such a divine sight under the brilliant sun's breath
   Is his garment d'or glittering ever since his imperial birth.
His crown soars sky high, for this earth does not deserveth.

The caretaker toils and sweats for the King's glitzy grind,
   And the arresting succulent dazzles the sun blind,
Unaware of the gloomy dark fate heading in the wind.

In the twilight, the caretaker swiftly draws an arc in the sky.
   And tumbling down the air of applause and ghastly glee
Is the magnificent head of a pineapple named Louie.

PASSING THOUGHTS

THE BLOWS

Beyond the fleeting Valley of Sorrows and Mournful Tears,
Greets the everlasting blows of the kindred spirits' laughter.

AGE UPON AGES

Season after season,
    Age makes mockery of the old and young.
The old fears time has gone too far
    Whilst the young fears time stands too long.

"But listen to me," the old says,
    "Beneath the ravenous and tough hide,
My merry adolescent heart discreetly steals
    The thrills and thunder of the past,
Withstanding shame or regret."

"But listen to me," the young say,
    "Beneath the buttery milk hide,
My all-knowing heart proudly trumps
    The thrills and thunder of the future,
Withstanding shame or regret."

Age upon ages, it has no shame or regret.
    Age says, "Listen to me, old and young.
I am just humble numbers
    Without any motive, intent, or desire.
Cherish me with gladness and readiness,
    For I am here to stay.
Spread thy wings of thrills and thunder,
    And ride the wind beneath
Without shame or regret."

THE END OF LIBERTY

In the undertaker world,
  Twice measured thoughts and gagged tongues
Exercise with caution and fear,
  Not to provoke ambushed anxiety and anger
In the cave of Pan and the den of lions.

A memory of the just and righteousness
  Of the old wise are no more
As rabid chaos and lunatics
  Dance high and wild,
Stumping the reminisce of
  Ancient grace to naught.

The echo of a mighty crimson guillotine
  Drowns the moaning and groaning
Of the honorable heads in the deep red.
  The lovely moon-lit dew on her blade
Now trickles like mournful tears
  Endlessly drowning the memory lane.

Woe unto the suckling of innocence!
  For the fair lady of Liberty weeps
For empty milk vessels.
  Woe unto the feeble minds and spirit!
For these are the beginnings
  Of vanishing hope and faith.

THE END OF AN ERA

The ancient wisdom of common sense
  Is of yesterday.
But now the newly discovered babble of non-sense
  Is of today.

The courageous defenders of free thinking and speaking
  Have now gone astray
As the reckless babes of endless garbles and shrieking
  Are here to stay.

The mute, dumb and deaf of yesterday
  Have not seen such an age
Since the mimes, parrots, and puppets of today
  Have taken the center stage.

Follies and destruction are now the rage
  As the old man of wisdom and prophecy
Are written off the page.

The quintessential teachers, thinkers, and orators
  Have been taken up in heavenly rapture,
And the disciples of confusion, lies and disorders
  Have taken over instead of their stature.

Woe unto you all, the rulers of the earth,
  For the truth of all ages has now become slander.
Woe unto you all, inhabitants of the earth,
  For the age of awakening has arrived in its deadly slumber.

TOO---Y

When the kisses of young lovers melt like cheese on top of pie,
  They said, "It is so heavenly."
The pie said to the lovers, "It is also too cheesy."

When the spirit of young lovers swooned over moonlight,
  They said, "It is so dreamy."
The moon said to the lovers, "It is also too early."

When the fingers of young lovers adorned the eternal rings,
  They said, "It is so lovely."
The ring said to the lovers, "It is also too easy."

When the days of marriage of young lovers flew by,
  They said, "It is so peachy."
The marriage said the lovers, "It is also too hasty."

When the souls of young lovers embraced together in the deep,
  They said, "It is so by and by."
The deep said to the lovers, "It is also too melancholy."

AT THE LIGHT

At high noon on the hottest day,
   The mighty hearts of valorous men and women were
Planted on either side of the valley
   Like a sea of tombstones with no names.

Only the sound of a whistling wind remained
   In the burnt, crimson, concrete forest.
A scent of stale phosphorus air filled heavy lungs
   And the faint scent of a trampled wildflower was lost
   forever.

The ardent souls waited for a great sign,
   A sign of perished or prevailed souls.
Some looked up, saw the birds in the air, and wished for
their wings.
   Some looked down and saw mangled flowers under their
   feet,
And melancholy memories flooded their spirits.
   Some saw their own ghosts on the other side of the valley,
Laughing haughtily, but without a sound.

Suddenly, a flash of emerald air abounds in the field,
   And a great wave of disturbance breaks the sea of staleness.
'Twas the sign they all have been waiting for ages.

A great excitement of relief and anxiety shouted,
    They marched faster, and faster, for the victory was nigh.
Much misery was conquered and denied this day.
    But soon their feet trampled upon each other, and
    hysteria climaxed
As the emerald light suddenly turned zircon and ruby once
again.
    Disheartened souls screeched and cried in great wrath
    and sorrow.

The wounded souls in the field gathered and stood
    Like a sea of tombstones with no name,
Waiting for the next great sign to continue their journey.

FOR WHOM THE BELL TOLLS

In the early dawn of Spring,
  The rustic bell in the house of rock tolls.

Clank and clank for
  Joyful sounds of acclamation and adoration.
Cry and cry for
  The babe born of ebbs and swells
Of pain and suffering known.

Clank and clank for
  Euphoric sounds of tender kisses at the altar.
Sigh and sigh for
  The waves of tremulous discords and heartaches,
Erases the happy memory of the wedding.

Clank and clank for
  Sleepy heads on another day of hard labor.
Groan and groan for
  The mind is willing, but the flesh is weak,
For the whips of the taskmaster awaits.

Clank and clank for
  Somber spirits mourn for the departed.
Joy and joy for
  The new dawn of Glory in Heavens
Where no bells clank and clank.

"For whom the bell tolls?"
  Asks the rustic bell in the house of rock
In the early dawn of Winter.

HOW WILL YOU KNOW?

The coolness of the brushing wind
    Without the strings of sweat.

The sweetness of a honeycomb
    Without the bitter stings of bees.

The sound of raindrops on a leaf
    Without the thunder clouds gathering.

The scent of a Spring morning
    Without the tilling of the earth.

The blazing love of a summer day
    Without the somber wintery night.

The sight of a starry sky
    Without the blackness of the night.

The angelic slumber of an afternoon
    Without Maxi's wee-hour morning fuss.

How will you know?

MOMENTS

Ambitious Moments traveled
   Too fast, too far and too much
In the fast lane.
   Time and seasons lamented for these moments,
Wishing them to be delayed.
   For the fleeting Moments,
Journeying carelessly
   Till the stumbling blocks
Of regret and guilt,
   Summoned are the furious drinks of shame and grief.

The heavy-hearted Moments,
   In the hands of Father Time,
Wiped the tears of content sore.
   In the bosom of Mother Season,
The Moments were comforted to a sweet slumber.
   As they watched other fleeting moments
Flashing by like a madman on the run,
   Like there is no time or seasons,
The spent Moments earnestly wished them to take a moment

To stop and linger.

POETRY FOR A DEAD SOCIETY

Palmist, not to be confused with Psalmist,
    Reads the soul as it adheres to its destiny,
And its certain journey awaiting at the end.

The mystic words of the palmist dazzle the eyes in the
hearts of fools.
    The gory painting becomes a fantastic abstract
    masterpiece,
To hide the works of dreadful woe, mockery of demonic toils
    And the path to the field called Golgotha.

The elites of a dead society treasure the babbles of the
palmist
    In the core of the soul, and magnify the works of self,
A closet full of skeletons and blackened blood of the
innocent.

Yea, the merry drink and meat are for the dead
    As their insidious workings glorify the depth of Hades.
One more riddle and conundrum before the sunrise,
    Before the light reveals the truth of their destiny.

UNTIL TOMORROW

One lonely evening of May,
   After ninety winters pass,
My heavy eyes see a glimpse
   Of a shadowy ghost of the past passing by.

My withered winter hands reach out
   To take his ghastly hand in my firm hold,
To take my pitiful soul out of this world.
   But even the ghost abhors the sight of mine,
For he stands silent, watching me from a distance.

Tonight, we sit together in the sound
   Of the dips and rises of my heartstrings
Until Lady Morrow encourages the ghost
   To take my hand and bring me home at last.

ONE OF THE SENSES

It is first to appear, and last to disappear.
   Upon receiving it, it is either for life or death.
It showers like a spring sunshine on the blessed souls,
   Or it mauls souls like a savage with blood caked talons.
Like a two-edged sword, it ravages souls once bitten.
   Blessed be the Lord for His words of mercy and salvation,
For we have no excuse twice as much or less, waxed with pride.
   Lest it runs through the canal and is lost forever in a river of murmurs.
Who am I?

THE SECRET FOREST OF BAMBOO

The ominous fortress of Bamboo stands afar.
 Only invited are the winds of the humble and meek,
Carefully treading the airs of discretion.

Whispers and murmurings of shadowy spirits,
 Hiding amongst the spears of giant stalks,
Are ever ready to sell the secrets of immortality.

Who will dare to seek and buy the glory of vanity?
 All but whose souls found the God of grace,
For the lost haughty souls still wonders the forest.

Finding the earthworms as its heirs,
 Vanity gnashes teeth and breathes death,
Buried amongst the secrets and glory of the earth.

THE FLIGHT OF ARROGANCE

How far up does arrogance fly?
Enough to be burned to the ground.

ONE DAY. . .

One day,
　The Normal said,
"Only if we could fly."
　The Subnormal said,
"We can try with our arms."
　The Abnormal said,
"Why use arms when you have legs?"
　The Normal said,
"Just try."

One day,
　The Normal said,
"Two plus two equals four."
　The Subnormal said,
"I think two plus two equals five!"
　The Abnormal asked,
"Plus? Why not minus?"
　The Normal said,
"Try again."

One day,
　The Normal said,
"The earth is a sphere."
　The Subnormal said,
"But it has four corners."
　The Abnormal said,
"Because it is flat."
　The Normal said,
"No comment."

One day,
The Normal says,
"I am called the Normal."
The Subnormal says,
"I feel like the Normal."
The Abnormal says,
"I am the New Normal."
The Normal weeps
Because of its becoming.

IN THE HOUSE OF CARDS

In the House of Cards, the walls have ears
   Of a murderous gale of gossip and murmuring,
Cutting and piercing souls a thousand times over.

Inside these walls is the Hall of Shame,
   Choked with heirs of venomous serpents,
Devouring each other to their end.

When Greed opens the door, Death walks in.
   When Pride opens the door, Hell walks in.
In the House of Cards, the walls have ears.

CAUTION AHEAD

Handle with care.
My ego gets bruised easily.
My head is full of emptiness.
I am pronoun sensitive,
And I have a superior bias.
Do as I say, not as I do.
Guilty until proven innocent

BOUNTY FOR THOUGHTS

Where have you gone this time, my dear?
     To your past or to the future?
To your dreams or nightmares?

Like whirlwind sand in an hourglass,
     So are the days of mine
Bound by a so-called life.

But you, my dear, are free as the wind
     Beyond borders and walls,
And the yoke of bondage,

Resting on hope and despair,
     Entertaining joy and anguish,
Wrestling courage and fear,

To ravage my soul and spirit,
     Like a two-edged sword,
Breaking bones and marrow.

Nonetheless, my dear, come hither.
     My eyes shall light the path
Of your flight back to me, I pray you,

For I am like dust in the air
     Without you, without your shadow
Of thoughts and doubt.

THE LILY OF THE VALLEY

Little one, how do you
   Breathe the souls of the earth,
And intoxicate the heavenly dew?

Little one, how can you
   Waltz in such flair
And serenade grace one stem at a time?

Little one, how mightily you
   Command the Sun and Moon,
And conquer the winds and mist!

Little one, how may you
   Grow and blow
In the hearts of desolation.

Little one, how I desire
   Your caress and whisper,
And your scent of redemption.

In the Valley of Lilies,
   I shall be like the little one,
Pure, carefree, and triumphant.

WHY MINE?

My precious one,
   My perfect partner in crime (of passion),
And my soulmate.

Why precious? One may ask.
   Then consider these things,
Much love of self, and is he/she not the other half ?

Why the perfect crime partner? One may mock.
   Then consider these things:
A needle with a thread, and bees with flowers

Why a soulmate? One may ponder.
   Then consider these things:
Two peas in a pod, and two sides of the coin.

LIVE FREE

A starry sky and a lake full of sparkle gems
 Entice the young souls of August
Into the naked twilight adventure.

Like a fish just discovering water,
 The lads ravage the brilliant blue,
Free from all cares and worries of the world.

It would be a night to remember the place
 Where the blithe spirit dwells
Because the crippling life's fate forbids such nostalgia.

Let not cruel reality besiege the soul!
 But rather the soul seizes the demonic plights
Of the dreams of the innocent and free.

YOUR MINDS

"Empty your mind,"
  One religion whispers
With no remedy for the void.

"Fill your mind!"
  One religion shouts
With no void to fill.

True religion teaches
  To empty the old soul of Sin
And to fill the void with the new Spirit.

In the days of shallow happiness and
  Deep sorrow, may your minds
Be at peace.

SOMEDAY,

Someday,
   I will banish myself
Into the wild of the South
   To squander the bright sunshine.

Someday,
   I will wrap myself
With a misty rain veil
   Without shame or loathing.

Someday,
   I will dance myself
To a ballad of Auroras
   Or a symphony of shooting stars.
Someday,
   I will fly myself
With the winds of Autumn
   To gather all the colors.

Someday,
   I will acquaint myself
With the sound of solitude
   And be content.

Until then,
   I will march boldly
To the day when Someday
   Becomes Today.

ONE LAST JOURNEY

An old man sat before the fire,
   And told a tale of a weary traveler
Who has ventured all corners of the world,
   Who also has walked the crowns of the earth,
And the belly of the ocean.

The ragged traveler also told
   The old man there is no more places
To see except for one.
   The old man asked, "Where?"
The traveler solemnly replied, "Six feet under."

MY DEAR DARLINGS

A corridor of ancient stone walls were children
    Laughed, cried, shouted, and whispered,
Chasing the distant dreams of hope, happiness, fame, and
fortune.
    Now, it is just a passage for the wind, birds, and night
    creatures.
Where have they gone, my dear darlings?

In the melting pot of concrete mazes and mayhem,
    The grindings and creaking of machineries
Drowned the toiled and downhearted marching
    Of the worker ants, bees, rats and deplorables,
As they are called, with a few pennies in their death clasps.

The battered and broken wails of the children,
    Carrying the shattered dreams of yesteryears
In the bosom of crimson-stained scars and blights,
    Were bottled up in their parched throats.
The words pitied them and retreated in somber silence.

By the ancient stones walls is a quiet passage of
bittersweet homecoming.
    The familiar scent of sweet and savory memories
Quickly wipe away the footprints of the vicious masters of
the world
    On their tattered spines, bruised skulls, and numbed spirits,
Like a furious sea ripples covering all traces of afflictions.

Ah, the shadows of joy are now traced on the ancient stone walls
  Of a merry go round carrying the prodigal sons and daughters.
The echoes of yesteryears etched in the crevices of the rocks,
  And their inhabitants are perplexed with a new sight.
Where have they come from, my dear darlings?

I AM SO SORRY

I am sorry my little one...
  I was too busy stuffing my own fat belly
  While your belly hung by the fangs of a hungry beast
    Because you were just an amusement in a game.

I am sorry my little one...
  I was too busy blabbing to the world
  While your parched throat was smothered shut
    Because you were voiceless, nonetheless.

I am sorry my little one...
  I was indulging my own eyes with lust
  While the claws of my lasciviousness ripped out your tender rib cages
    Because you were just a loathsome creature.

I am sorry my little one...
  I was too afraid of my own sin's long shadow
  While your tiny bones and skull found comfort in the deep
    Because you were really a stumbling block.

I am sorry my little one...
  Someday, I too shall suffer the consequences
  While your languishment, lamentation, and woe echo in my core
    Because you were the innocent one.

THE WHITE CATHEDRAL

Once the nightcrawlers and worms
    Embellish their bellies and essence,
The white relic of the mortal squirms
    Silently in the shallow offence
Of rain and shine, dawn and dusk, and war and peace.
    Then the angel of jest discovers its piece
And, by and by, the cathedral rallies.

The White Cathedral becomes a masterpiece,
    Adorning the house of heavenly worship,
As the marvelous skulls and bones coil and heap.
    Pilgrims of all nations came in a sweep,
Forgetting their own destiny of the skin deep.
    Thus is the awesome display of fallacy,
Confounding the angel of Jest who lost his fancy.

MY JEALOUS ARCHFOE

If only my jealous archfoe were a mumchance
   Whilst my maddening rampage,
Visited the misguided menace,
   Then the holy union of strife and rage
Would not have provoked my peace.

If only my jealous archfoe were blind
   Against all my futile principles and substance
Of all carnal flesh, blood, and mind,
   Then the reaping and heaping of imprudence
Would not have suffered my mind in a diabolic wind.

If only my jealous archfoe were deaf
   On the showers of murmurs and discords,
Ready to flood the field of mischief,
   Then the bemused parade of gnawers
Would not have drowned my soul in grief.

If only my jealous archfoe was not so zealous
   Of my doing, of my being, and of my lore,
And be content with my flawed status,
   Then my own worst foe and grievance no more.
But, together, we are indeed murderous.

WHEN THE SKY FALLS

The sky's the limit
    When it comes to the cloud's outfits,
Morphing and changing, conjuring tricks in the sky
    Every second, hour and day.

So are the obsessive minds of self-lovers,
    The best version of self every second, hour and day.
Such is the father of lies and deception,

Who fell through the sky,
    Bringing his filth to the earth.
The whole world conforms to his will,
    And to the maddening spirits of self-lovers.

Deceiving its prey with the Lily of the Cobra
    Out of an open sepulcher, the words of sweet poison,
The honeyed tongue of a death trap crushes its victim.

The tickling ears, waxed hard against the innocent cry,
    Are drowned by the echoes of demonic laughter
Until the sky falls.

A new sky and earth unveil
    The innocent blood and flesh rejoicing,
For redemption has come to their aid.

The winds of justice break and chase
    The clouds of menace and confusion
Down the deep sewer where they belong.

There, the gnashing teeth and claws
    Of the self-lovers consume each other
Every second, hour and day.

THE WILD YONDER

Garnished with cobwebs, my crown of vanity
  Dangles from this withered reality
Of a feeble old soul with long shadows of mortality,
Once lionhearted, and of brutality.

It desperately waves the fleeting time for an audience
  From the edge of the dead-end indulgence.
Nay, says the time, as it flies off to the wild yonder
  While the timekeeper's rein keeps it tight under.

This unfortunate squandered time of mine
  Wastes not a journey to the finish line.
Leaving trails of stinging regret and wails,
  My dusty crown at last hails the coffin nails.

SPIRITUAL

DIRT

An earthen vessel made of dirt are we.
    What is there to hope?
To be beaten and broken?

Are we all just dust in the air
    To wander to nothingness? Nay.

Let us embrace and hold firm
    The sacred life-giving seed,
Even the mustard seed,
    With grace and mercy.

Let the seed take refuge
    In our innermost chamber
To be nourished and strengthened.

Let the fruit of every kind
    Be of a thirst quenching, savory aroma,
Pleasing in sight and touch,
    To be lovely, joyous, peaceful, kind,
Patient, good, faithful, gentle
    And self-sacrificial.

Let us not forget the life of the earth,
    But remember the end of that life
Of dirt with a glorious gift, and much reward.

Are we all just a wanderlust in the air?
    "Nay, nay, nay,"
As Heaven protests.

THE OLD MAN

A lone old stonewall stands majestic
   In the valley of no name,
Withstanding the whips of rainy winds
   From every direction and season.

Chasing away the youth and gallantry of all names,
   The stonewall of deep battle wounds, calluses, and scars
Proudly displays the fallen conquest of endless foot prints
   Until the thick dust carpet covers the trails of a triumph.

One day, a seducing spirit of brilliant thistle and thorn
   Beguiles the lonely battered old stonewall,
Promising an exquisite garment
   Of eternal beauty and awesome terror.

A fallen prey becomes the stonewall of no name,
   Crowned with thorns and devoured by vanity and pride.
Fallen as a discarded ruin of a forgotten ancient hero,
   Fallen as I, the Old Man.

ENDEAVOR

Will there be showers of Spring endeavor
    In the field of stolen souls of men?

When the sun rises again
    Upon the field without pride and prejudice,
And when the sky weeps for the lost ones
    As the field embraces its tears
With repentance and thanksgiving,

Then, "Yes," the wind of the West replies
    With hope and mercy at bay.

SO, IT BEGINS

In the land of sorrows, a weeping bride mourns
Of her sunrises and sunsets for His return.

Once a bright eyed forever,
    Raven hair adorned with spring delights,
The blushing bride fluttered the hearts of all shapes and
forms.
    Now, the eyes are shut dim,
And her white straw hair hugs the ground
    As her contorted frail shell
Frightens even the wild street dogs.

Her bride's dress of tears tatters in the wind
    Like the merciless whips of a brute.
When her frozen fingers reach for heaven,
    Her wails of despair echo a thousand years.
Only the silence of the dead winter returns
    To taunt her soul and body for thousands and
    thousands of years.

Near the edge of darkness,
    The trembling bride sees a spirit.
Soon, on her eyes and upon her sweet life,
    A dark cloud and thick blackness descend
To embrace the shuddering mortal.

So, it begins.
    The bride's stern eyes are like aflame candles
Of everlasting warmth and brilliance.
    Her pearly hair now adorns the crown of gems
As her radiant smile dazzles the stars of galaxy,
    And her glorious gown garment flows in the air for aye.

Her tears of joy are wiped away
    In His tender embrace of infinity.
The bride's fervent soul
    Of love unspeakable, unquenchable, and unforgettable
Conquers the iniquity beyond this world and the next.

Her frozen smile silences the world
    As the dogs lick off her frost stiffen corpse ever
    more warm.
All is ready for the lonely funeral
    In the land of sorrow and perdition.

So, it begins.
    The wedding feast of the heavenly bride,
Hailed with compassion and faith,
    Proclaims her holy matrimony
And echoes forever in the heavens
    As the angels' velvety wings wash off her feet
With myrrh and frankincense.

The sound of a blushing bride's feet
    On the streets of gold and precious gems,
And the chorus of heavenly bodies
    Silence the wailings of the earthlings
For ten thousand years and beyond.

The heavenly blushing bride looks down
    From above with a jubilant smile
As the memory of her flickers
    Like a candle of turmoil and troubledness,
And the worms of the earth feast
    On her body.

OPIATES FOR THE MASSES

Religion is like
    Opiates for the masses,
Inducing false happiness and hope,
    And numbness to truth and reality,
For Religion is man-made
    Works of pride and prejudice,
And wages of guilt and torment.
    For all the failures and disappointments,
What must men do?
    Take Opiates for now?

Christianity is standing on the promises
    Of the One from above
In love, light, and life,
    And believing in what
He has done already.
    The work of grace rests on
Eternal peace, hope and joy
    By the river of the true opiate
From the fountain on the golden street.

IN THE WOMB

As I lay dreamless alone
   In the glorious midsummer's night,
I hear the wind of a faint heart
   In the ancient timbers of this house,
Or is it the ghosts murmuring in the dungeons?

My bone shivers of an ominous
   Storm brewing in the sea nearby,
Or is my soul trembling at the sight
   Of the death angel's white coattail?

As a burning sea wind's scream grows,
   So does the shadows of the beast.
Its dragon's talons creep closer,
   Slowly chafing my flesh,
And gnawing my soul to nought
   Without mercy and tears.
My refuge has become my sepulcher.
   My soul is no more, no more
Like dew drop from a grass,
   And like ash in terrible winds.

Then I remember the water,
   Womb of mine, ocean of peace,
As its tender ripples caress my head
   Like a never-ending heavenly dream.

I hear the gentle voice
        Calling my name, my soul,
Promising an eternal world
        And a heaven at my feet.
He knows my name,
        And the numbers of my hair,
For I am His and His forever.

I cry out to Him, Him alone,
        "Save me, Save me!"
He wipes the tears away and says,
        "My sweet child, I have, I am, and I will. Always."

ELDORADO

The Wide gate, adorned with gold garnishment and tinsel,
        Enticed the earthly souls with gold dust sprinkle.

A gate so wide and splendid,
        Many bewitched and blinded.
As a token of wages, their souls bonded.
        'Twas for the frantic masses,
A promise of Eldorado for all that passes.

Beyond the gate were the dark mysteries
        Unknown behest to greediest creatures.

Some fell into the deep forest bottoms,
    Making a merry feast for earthworms,
And, robbed of their robe of righteousness,
    Became ashes of nothingness,
Ever wandering for Eldorado in the darkness (even now).

The Narrow gate, adorned with vultures, thistles, and thorns,
    Was of a sore despot, disgust, and despise.

Till a meek and humble pilgrim of ancient Grace
    Testified that the Narrow is the way, truth, and life.
Free to enter, just deny the world and all its glory.
    A few dared to believe and trust his story.
Of the few, some crawled through the entry.

Beyond the Narrow gate was the Valley of Shadows and
Sorrows,
    A truly frightening sight of utter horrors.

Some wondered if they should have taken the gate so wide
    Till a white spirit offered his hand to guide
While the sweet hour carried them aloft like a cherished
bride.
    Ah, at last! The streets of gold, the Eldorado, were
    beneath the feet of wings
As the homecoming trumpet sounded its blessings upon
the be loved.
    Bathed in the golden lights, the bride rested in the
    bosom of the Holy One
Of eternal peace, love, and glory.

THE RULER OF THE NIGHT

As the sun retreats below the horizon,
    The darkness stretches its wings.
Lurking and stalking is the shadow
    Of a hideous creature of the night
Who cloaks himself in the misty wintery fog.
    Only the blazing eyes of hell,
And a demonic grin with dragon fangs
    Dipped in the boiling poisonous blood
Creep into the lair of godly men
    To churn their meat and blood for a feast.

Behind the mighty iron gates and ways,
    Mettle men awaken, standing still and waiting.
The unchecked atrocity of their doom
    Will plunge the souls and spirits
Into the deepest of the deep in the core of the fiery bath
    Where their kinsmen laid since the terror stroked.
They pray the Lord, their King and Captain,
    Their death may be quick and bring honorable funerals,
For they fight and perish in the name of God,
    For the beast is the enemy of God and His.

But the Almighty God is the ruler
    Of the day and night, good and evil,
And He has chosen the victor for His sake.
    This night, the godly men shall see
The hands of God rip apart and crush
    The shadow stalker into the oblivion and beyond.
As the dawn breaks, behold, the reminisce of the beast
    In the field before the iron gates of the lair.
The only shadows are the fowls of the air circling
    To feast on the beastly death of the Fallen one.

LIFE IN THE CRACK LANE

Once a green pasture with springs for an ole grove,
  Now is a melted molten rock for the carriages of men.
No tears for the birds in the air, or the crawlers of the earth,
  Or for the forest dwellers of day and night.

The Sun's rays of wrath beat down the molten rock.
  In hiding are the shadows of comfort and rest.
Day by day is the merciless sweltering and sweating of the
rock
  Until a small crack opened in the earth.

All quiet and cautious souls await in the lane.
  The tears of heaven and earth trickle down,
Awaiting the blessings of Heaven, the ruler of all.
  Behold, a single bold weed overcomes the darkness
With the glorious sunbeams of life and vitality.

The cracks seeped with a spirit of resilience and vigor,
  Now bringing forth hope and promise
Like showers of glory and redemption
  In furious winds of all directions.

Reigned in the land of melted molten rock,
  And reclaiming what was once theirs,
Are the well-watered green pasture of an ole grove,
  And the joyous spirits of earth dwellers.
Even so are the carriages of men.

THE HARVEST MOON

Her amber, angelic glee bewitches all living souls
    As she tiptoes into the autumn night sky.
Her breath is soft and cool, easing any pain of a hard day's
labour.
    Serenading admirers under her window
Makes the timekeeper slumber in heavenly peace.
    These are the times of grace and mercy.

Waiting for the gleaning of the earthly souls,
    And picturing mayhem, she mourns the day.
Her toilsome breath is about to birth unbending pang
    As The timekeeper turns his key of eternity
Whether it would be for damnation or redemption.
    These are the times of judgment and penance.

As the new dawn's early light breaks,
    She takes a little glimpse of the night's reaping.
Her fluttered heart seizes one more breath again.
    The glorious sun rises upon the land of the precious
Souls gathered, ready present, before the Almighty.
    These are the days of new beginning and the end.

THE REDEEMER

From a distance,
   You knew my long and cursed shadow.
Howbeit, falling and kissing,
   My blackened neck and feet
You blessed over and over.
   Your tears of compassion
Washed away the filth of the world,
   And your velvety raven hair
Cradled my trembling naked flesh.

Sweet kisses and warm tears,
   All for the unfaithful one
Who has forsaken you, my dearest,
   For the lustrous world of the wicked
That undid mine at last.
   Disrobed of righteousness,
Betrayed and scourged,
   My soul and mortal body
Were ready to be devoured
   At the mouth of Hades.

Oh, how I longed for yours
   From the edge of this world!
The haunted memories of your love
   Pierced my bleeding heart all over again,
Groaned and mourned forever,
   In the inferno of sins
And tears of sorrowness.

Till a familiar shadow
      Of weeping and caressing
Blanketed my long shadow
      Of a dead man's folly,
Oh, how I much agonized
      For your kisses and embrace
Of forgiveness and mercy
      On the unfaithful one,
On the wretched one,
      On the undeserved one. Selah.

A DREAM IN A DREAM

I lay me down in the early evening
      As a fiery throb in my head raged.
My own spirit's breath fanned the fire
      So blazing that my poor soul fainted.

I saw the chilly moon hung on the limbs
      Of a somber darkness coming.
An unknown spirit seduced my wretched soul,
      Mystic, friendly at first, but turned violent at once.
Stinging in the ice river of suffering,
      My soul was then showered with his arrows of fury.

As my shuddered limbs chased the spirit's shadows
  Of the ebbs and billows of the ocean,
My soul descended into the fiery ice water.
  He was quick and cunning like the devil serpent.
He hid in the walls, slithering and coiling,
  And laughed his fangs in my face.
Frozen in spirit, my soul cried out
  Until a gentle soul pulled me out of the current.
My head, on the bosom of my sweet mate,
  Awakened, but the dreadful squirmy walls were still.
(Only for my eyes to see, and my soul to feel.)
  Tormented, I cried my soul out, but none comforted,
Even my sweet mate, my soul mate of eternal,
  Whispered that it was just a dream.

Then the claws of the serpent ripped the wall
  To deliver us both to a void, to sink us to the deep.
Frozen in spirit, my soul cried out.
  My sweet mate was in horror, in drippings
Of the poisonous vapors of the beast,
  Until a gentle soul pulled us out of the void.

My head, on the bosom of my sweet mate,
  Was awakened in his hands.
Washed off was the dew of pain and suffering
  As my soul mate whispered that it was just a dream.
The gentle moon beam casted a shadow,
  A shadow of wings of the heavenly one
Encircling my soul and spirit, my own spirit.
  It was just a dream in a dream.

THE BENEATH

Beneath the decks of gold and precious gems,
   And garments of adoration and praise
Are the dirty rags of dead blood.

Beneath the beguiling, sweet words of a fleshly soul,
   And empty praises of all manners
Are the cruel words of a murderous rant
   Of both the living and the dead.

Beneath the merry steps on the honorable street
   Of all nations and people
Are the catacombs of saints and heavenly ones.

Beneath the breath of fragrant roses and sea blue star
   Of the fat earth and ocean
Are the poisonous thorns of a certain harrowing affliction.

Oh, wretched men of the flesh, see, hear and taste!
   The entropy of the living corpses is ready to devour
The innocent, honorable and meek from within and without.

WAITING TO EXHALE

When I was born of a babe
   In this cruel world, out of the Lord's keeping,
My breath was afraid to exhale.
   So, I got my first gentle spank and cried.

When the love of my life
   Said love forever in this life and the next,
My breath remembered not to exhale.
   So, I stole a sweet breath from my love.

When the deaths of my loved ones
   Became of this world, from dust to dust,
My breath abhorred to exhale.
   So, I slumbered in lament to forget.

When death visited me one night,
   With no easy bargain to suffer,
My breath waited to exhale.
   So ready was I for the Lord's keeping once again.

GIFT OF TEARS

When memories of you appear in the frost-bitten night,
  My blistering heart flutters with bittersweet ardor.
The angels of slumber retreat, but those of melancholy do not.
  The absence of your spirit pounds my bones and marrow,
Even utterances of longing flee, leaving me with just cold
  tears.
No comfort for the soul nor the tears.

Oceans of tears, surging waves of wails and woes,
  Churns my soul, drowning my spirit into suffocation,
Into the depths of sorrow, and the lair of the devil's litter.

My tears of pity linger as my soul and spirit
  Pray the Lord for quickening mercy.
A gentle wind of solace brushes off the dew of angst,
  A reminder of your angelic touch.
It numbs my grief, sedates the angels of melancholy,
  And carries my weary and wrecked soul into blissful
  sleep once again.

DIRT UPON DIRT

Nothing is new under the sun.
  Such is the mortal soul and body encased in shells
Of all colors, shapes, and forms
  On loan from the Maker in Heaven.

Covered in gold threaded garments,
  Decked with precious gems and glitter,
Youthful age and strength boast their might and pride
  Like there is no end.

Walking on dirt of all kinds,
  Prideful men indulge much
In lustrous desires of heart and soul,
  Including immortality.

But the God of heaven and earth looks down,
  Mocking the dead men walking,
For his days are numbered without fail.
  The body that was lent will perish into dust,
And the soul will expire into the judgement, such is His will.

The bright eyes dim, the eloquent tongues dumb, the keen
ears dull,
  And merry hearts wax cold and hard
Like a flower bloom in the morning that fades in the
evening.
  Such is the mortal body and soul ready to expire.
A dreaded death will come to sweep them into the deep.

And the God of heaven and earth looks down,
    And pours wrath on the haughty spirits of men,
For they vent rage upon their own bane,
    Inflicting the harrow of Hades,
And ravaging their fellow souls into havoc and death.

Prideful men fill the fields of the earth
    With their own skulls and bones,
Dirt upon dirt, to be trodden under the feet of animals.
    Violent men bloody the water that surges and wallows
With loathsome gore and bloated corpses.

Woe unto thee, mortal body, soul, and spirit.
    Be kind to yourself and your kind,
For one lifetime is due any time and day.
    Cleave unto the heavenly One, the Creator.
Pray for mercy and peace upon thyself and each other.

ZERO TOLERANCE

Zero to sixty seconds gone.
    Zero pennies to a billion pennies.
Zero "Likes" to a million "Likes."

Earthlings boast in their status.
    They eat, drink and are merry
Like there is no season or time.

The Almighty laughs at the dead men boasting,
    For there is always a season, a time,
And zero tolerance for the sins of mortals.

ONE TWILIGHT NIGHT

When the last beam of sunlight flees,
  And the flickering flame of a candle expires at last,
The ominous wings of a menacing spirit stretch high
and wide,
  Out of its slumber and earthly gallery of mayhem.

With a demonic glee, the serpent's venomous fangs
  Await to strike a well of blood.
Its talons of gore-ready look for a fresh tormented soul
  To summon death to whoever is on his path of destruction.

The Lord of the dark skies flies from the mountain top to
the bottom of the ocean.
  The sky roamer steadies his God-cursed eyes on the lost
  soul of the night.
Dripping with pride and arrogance from the fire scorned
scales,
  The serpent takes a deep breath, swells his chest with a
  wind of wrath,
And swoops down to inflict his fatal blow on innocent soul
and flesh.

But the Keeper of the soul, the guardian of His children,
  Wields the shield of faith against the fiery darts of the
  storm.
Coiling, convulsing, and igniting hate as his battle fire
quenches,
  The unyielding serpent viciously races towards the
  poor soul.

But the infallible sword of the Mighty God draws an arc
  Into the belly of the Beast, weakening the fiery flame.
The bane of souls and the foe of mankind, broken and
bowed,
  Retreats into the molten rock of his death den,
Leaving behind the trails of broken crimson scales, and
smoldering darts.

The angel of the Lord takes the poor soul into his
celestial wings,
  And carries her through the twilight, away from the
  battlefield.
Tonight, a wretched death has been denied, and the
anguished sorrow has fled.
  The stretched arms of God of grace takes the trembling
  soul
Into the blissful dawn of a new day, and a merciful embrace
of eternal love.

For Malia. 04/26/2021

ALMOST

Almost in the grasp of Shangri-La,
   My eyes search for the familiar breath,
A shallow breath resting on a thin line.

So close yet so far from eternity,
   Fervent tears of hope and sorrow
Now stir the torrid lake of fire.

Almost in the grasp of the winged angels,
   My hands roam the heavens
For a runaway feather once again.

So close yet so far from eternity,
   The angels escape my grip of desperation
Like sand running through my fingers.

Almost persuaded unto salvation,
   My soul sails on troubled waters
Like a lost sheep in a den of wolves.

I AM

I am that He is.
    Created him for me,
And I for him.

When the King of Time
    Visits me in the darkest hour,
I shall shed tears of farewell.

Tears of gladness and sorrow descend,
    Mingled with his and mine,
Until the Lord wipes away all.

I am that He is,
    Oneness in Spirit,
Forever and ever.

THE ARK

The gift of the Ole Grace
    Is the Ark of eternal salvation,
Deemed by the Creator of all.

Safely nested in the sanctuary,
    Carried away in Love,
Mortal souls shall not want.

In the midst of traitorous storms,
    The divine Light guides the soul
Onto the path of Righteousness and Truth.

Smooth sailing or not,
    The sanctified life, the conqueror of death
Overcomes the world and the serpent.

At the mouth of milk and honey river,
    The true journey of everlasting glory awaits
The destiny of the Ark.

ALMOST COMPROMISED

Unity!
 A so-called wise one shouts,
Not knowing the obvious.
 Water does not mingle with oil,
Compromising the substance of the two.

Unity!
 A so-called brave one shouts,
Afraid of the obvious.
 Light does not sleep with darkness,
Compromising the essence of the two.

Unity!
 A so-called leader of the world shouts,
Bewitching the obvious.
 Truth does not honor lies,
Compromising the integrity of the two.

Unity!
 A heavenly host shouts,
Blessing the obvious.
 The marriage of the Soul and Spirit,
A perfect end of the Two.

IF I COULD

If I could wash away yesterday's filth
   In the river of no return, and
Be purified by the sun kissed blessings of today,
   What an exhilarating day that will be!

If I could rescue all the little darlings of nefarious caves
   Unto the ultimate dream field to fly, run and tumble,
And hear their belly laughter and happy yells,
   What an illuminating feat that would be!

If I could savor the winds and mists
   Carrying all my beloved's scent and aura
Across the river Styx one more time,
   What an unfeigned feast that would be!

If I could converse about anything
   With my furry wild child of mine called Maxi
Without bribes or indulgences,
   What a jolly teatime that would be!

If I could fly around the galaxies
   With an army of hummingbirds,
And see the awe beauty of creation,
   What an exuberant adventure that would be!

If I could plant my head in my love's bosom
   To hear the heart strings' whale songs,
To hold unconditional love, and to fervent my soul forever,
   What a crowning moment that would be!

If I could tiptoe into my fairest dream,
  And bring back a little morsel to nibble
In the midst of despondent reality rampant,
  What a scrumptious treat that would be!

If I could tell a story about the gospels
  Of true Love, Life and Light,
And all the stars in the sky madly shouted "Amen!",
  What an intoxicating night that will be!

If I could....

I WILL

The fool hath said,
  "My body is my own
And I Will do whatever
  I want, need and must."

The wise answered and said,
  "My body is not my own,
For I created not the body,
  Nor labored or purchased it.

The mortal body lent from above,
  A perfect creation by the perfect Creator,
Until Sin corrupted the vessel.
  Thus, as dust, it shall return."

The fool hath said,
  "I have all the time in my hand
And I Will do whatever
  I want, need and must."

The wise answered and said,
  "I am on a borrowed time.
For I do not hold in my hand the key
  Of the Book of Life.

Behold the appointments
  With the Death Angel is at hand
To usher souls out of this world.
  The Timekeeper keeps His word."

The fool hath said,
  "I control my destiny
And I Will do whatever
  I want, need, and must."

The wise answered and said,
  "I do not know the future.
But I know whom I believe
  Holds my destiny.

The clay, an earthen substance,
  Is shaped, fired, and purposed by
The Master Potter of the universe.
  So shall the spirit surrender to His Will."

TO LIVE OR TO DIE

Live to die
    Is all about the living.
Every breath summons a validity
    Of excellent wine and meat,
And the virtue of prowess without fear and shame.
    A purpose-driven vanity without a lost cause,
Striving and taking it to the summit, is the glory of
mankind.
    These insipid words from a famished wolf of the wild
Inspire all to challenge and conquer the Game of the Living,
    To the end of life as food for worms in an evil hour.

Die to live
    Is all about the dying.
Every breath summons true wisdom
    Of winged words from heaven:
A wretched soul perishes in its own folly without excuse or
hope.
    But dying in Christ alone is the true beginning of the
    next life.
These spirited words from the humble sheep of the
wilderness
    Inspire all to challenge and conquer the Sting of Death
    once and for all,
To a glorious new life forever and ever in the sweet hour.

NOT ALONE

Solitude is not punishment,
  But is true freedom
From self and its realm,
  For none would claim
Wants, Needs and Sine Qua Non
  As a token of debt.

Solitude is never alone,
  But is joined by the conscience
And the subconscious of
  Both mortals and immortals.
A perfect balance of the mind and flesh
  As the sun is not without a shadow.

Solitude is an epitome of oneness:
  One mind, one soul, and one spirit.
Without solitude, chaos follows.
  Embrace the solitude,
For it is the way to true salvation
  In the Father, Son and Holy Spirit.

THE BLESSED

My eyes shall not well up
　　For lost earthly materials:
Time, seasons, pleasures, and vanity,
　　For these are substances of the cursed.

But my spirit shall drown in the wailing sea
　　For the loss of a dearly beloved,
Heavenly voices of Love, Life and Light,
　　For these are the treasures of the blessed.

All the cares of the world
　　Abound in vanity and strife.
All soon to be six feet under, a spoil for worms.
　　Such is the way and end of carnal souls.

But my redeemed soul shall not want
　　From here to eternity.
An inheritance of all manifestation,
　　For I am a child of the Almighty.

THE KEY TO MY HEART

Like a flickering candlelight in the fury-fed wind,
    So is this perilous life of the contrite.
But my shivering heart outshines the sun's pride,
    Searching for the long-lost key
Once encased in the sanctuary,
    Chamber of all zeal and glory
Of yesterdays, todays, and tomorrows.

In my green youth, I traded the key
    For the spoils of the world,
But was robbed by the lord of deception.
    As a shattered feeble spirit, I become a castaway.
An empty keyhole's shadow rippled
    As my haunted ghost battled
The ocean of the troubled and wounded.

But Mercy and Hope confounded
    My old soul and its counterpart.
Arising above the waxed heart,
    A fire seed called Grace
And the breath of a new race
    Fanned the smoldering smokes,
Deepening the rage and wrath of redemption.

Forged in the terrible inferno of Love,
    A new key wades into the depths
Of the forgotten and incarcerated
    Until grief is consummated.
No soul or spirit can ever gnaw away
    The key anchored to my core:
All forgiven, forgotten, and promised.

REST THY TOILED SOUL

Come, come now, and rest thy toiled soul
    On a cool evening bed of ambrosial slumber.
Let thine eyelids be heavy laden with anisole,
    And angelic songs of luminous amber.

For the sun queen's fiery chariot and whips stand steady,
    But the celestial maiden proclaims her starry sky.
Let the sweetened dreams of heavenly milk and honey
    Nurse thy beaten and broken spirit, and wholly satisfy.

For the hard labour and grief-stricken tomorrow is wrought
    Whether a battle-ready soul is or not.
The taskmaster's fists and rods are ever assiduously sought.
    As under the sun, nothing is discreet.

CPSIA information can be obtained
at www.ICGtesting.com
Printed in the USA
LVHW082201290422
717576LV00013B/281